A Scientist Asks a Ground Zero Pastor

WHERE WAS GOD ON SEPTEMBER 11?

JOHN HORGAN
and
the Reverend FRANK GEER

SAN FRANCISCO
BROWNTROUT PUBLISHERS

Library of Congress Control Number: 2002141450

Library of Congress Cataloging-in-Publication Data is available.

Entire contents © 2002 BrownTrout Publishers, Inc.
Text © 2002 John Horgan and Francis H. Geer
Cover photographs © 2002 Jaanika Peerna

P.O. Box 280070
San Francisco, California 94128
U.S.A.

CONTENTS

PREFACE

The five hijackers of American Airlines Flight 11 out of Boston Logan International Airport gained control of the cockpit of the Boeing 767 fifteen minutes into flight. They flew the plane west to Amsterdam, New York, where they turned abruptly south to follow the Hudson River down to New York City. Fifty-five miles north of the city, Flight 11 almost collided with the second hijacked airliner out of Logan: United Airlines Flight 175, which was crossing the Hudson River from east to west en route to a southerly approach on Lower Manhattan.

At this moment of near collision, the hijackers saw before them the scenic gorge that the Hudson River cuts through the Appalachian Mountains—and, sitting in the heart of the gorge, the United States Military Academy. So transparent was the air of that beautiful September morning that the hijackers might even have descried the roof of a certain house on a wooded hillside facing West Point across the river, under which sat an author putting the finishing touches on his book about spirituality and science.

Arriving a minute later at the southern end of the gorge, the hijackers of Flight 11 saw below them the twin domes of Indian Point nuclear power plant. Passing up these two points of interest, the hijackers kept the plane on its downriver course and six minutes later drove it into the North Tower of the World Trade Center. At the moment of impact, the rector of the Episcopal church in the hamlet in which the author lived sat drinking a cup of coffee with his elderly father in a Manhattan apartment. Within minutes, the pastor was rushing to report to the emergency room of the big city hospital where he worked as director of religious services. Within minutes, the author and his wife were running breathlessly to the top of the hill behind their house, from which on a clear day they could see the Twin Towers.

This book is a conversation between the pastor and the science writer about September 11. The pastor is the Reverend Frank Geer, rector of St. Philip's Church-in-the-Highlands in Garrison, New York. The science writer is the noted author and intellectual gladiator, John Horgan. Frank and John are friends and neighbors with a long history of polemical conversation behind them. Two people more unalike in station or opinion can scarcely be imagined. Yet the priest and the scientist proved to share a pleasure in verbal skirmish and philosophical combat, regulated by mutual respect and driven by mutual curiosity.

This odd couple started and continued their conversation in a little country store attached to the train station at Garrison's Landing, the old ferry slip across the water from West Point. At the back of the store, behind a dusty stack of custard powder and oatmeal biscuits, is hidden a snug solarium poised precariously over the to-and-fro of the river's tidal currents. Here the rector would take sanctuary from his pastoral duties to sip his coffee and read the morning papers while waiting for the train to take him to his weekday job at St. Luke's–Roosevelt Hospital. Here, too, the local literary lion would pad in for a splash of caffeine-laced relief from the reclusion of his writing den deep in the forest. Word traveled through the highlands that a lively back-and-forth about ultimate matters might often be overheard in the early morning hours at the back of the old store at the Garrison train station. The pastor might miss his train; the writer might miss his deadline: the great conversation rolled on and on.

After September 11, 2001, the conversation stopped for a while. Reverend Geer was working extra-duty at the hospital, counseling and comforting survivors of the attacks on the World Trade Center, families of the victims, and rescue workers. When the conversation resumed just before Thanksgiving, its recurring themes—the nature of truth, the problem of evil, the human need for meaning, the risks to humanity inherent in human yearnings for certainty—had all assumed a new relevance and urgency.

As a neighbor overhearing snatches of this famous ongoing conversation, I had been struck by the intellectual mettle and humane wisdom of both speakers. But I was even more impressed by the readiness of each one to look critically at the boundaries of his own world-view without abandoning its core doctrine. These rarely combined qualities of confidence, tolerance, and daring seemed to infuse their conversation with a dialectical energy that freely experimented with tentative syntheses. Both men were stretching themselves toward the promise of a more evolved, convergent understanding.

I asked John and Frank if they would consider having one of their cracker-barrel conversations taped, transcribed, and published for the benefit of those who have, in the wake of September 11, been troubled by the very questions that have long preoccupied the two of them. They consented, on condition that their royalties go to charity.

Robert Hutchinson
Editor

I
WHERE WERE YOU ON SEPTEMBER 11?

WHERE WERE YOU ON SEPTEMBER 11?

John Horgan: Frank, where were you when you first heard about the attacks on the World Trade Center?

Frank Geer: I was at my parents' apartment in New York City. I was talking with my father over coffee, and the *Today Show* was on in the background, when all of a sudden I saw that picture of the North Tower with smoke coming out of it. I said, "Hey, look at this." Then we saw the second plane hit. Thirty seconds later, I had my coat on and was heading up to St. Luke's Hospital on the Upper West Side, where I serve as the director of religious services. I'm supposed to go to the hospital during a crisis like this to deal with the victims and family members when they come in. The rest of that day, we were treating primarily firemen and policemen with smoke inhalation, burns, or broken bones. I served as a pastor to these people who'd been down at the site and listened to their stories.

So where were you on September 11, John?

John Horgan: I was at home in Garrison working on a book about science and spirituality. Around 8:30 or so that morning, my wife Suzie called me and said there was something on television that I should really see. So I left my office and went into the living room and started watching the TV just around the time the second plane hit. My wife and I watched the television for a half-hour or so, and then we suddenly decided to go to this hill near our home where you can see the Manhattan skyline. We ran through the woods to the top of this hill, and we looked south across the Hudson River to this notch in the hills where the Twin Towers had been visible, and you couldn't see them anymore. There was just smoke. We kept saying over and over that we couldn't believe this was happening.

Frank Geer: One thing that went through my mind early on was that scene from one of the *Star Wars* movies, right after the Death Star blows up that whole planet. It cuts to Obi-Wan Kenobi, who clutches at his chest and looks faint. Luke asks him, "What's the matter?" And Obi-Wan says, "I just heard the sound of thousands of voices all being suddenly silenced at the same moment."

John Horgan: Did any of the people you were counseling on September 11 ask you how God could have allowed this to happen?

Frank Geer: Nobody on that day asked where God was. They just hadn't reached that level of questioning yet. In a situation like that, what helps people is just being able to tell their story to someone who's willing to listen and who cares and maybe is going to hold them by the hand and give them a hug or just look them in the eye.

John Horgan: You've reminded me of something that Huston Smith once said to me. Smith is a religious scholar I interviewed for a book I'm writing on spirituality, called *Rational Mysticism*. He has a profoundly religious, optimistic view of the world. He believes in a God who loves us. So I asked him how he reconciled this belief with the Holocaust and children getting cancer. He gave me an answer about how God is infinite, and if something is infinite it must encompass all possibilities, including the possibility of evil. It was all very complicated, and finally Smith admitted that ultimately explanations like these are not very satisfying. Then he told me this story about a woman, a friend of his, who learned from a doctor that she was about to go blind. And afterwards she visited a minister and asked him how God could let this happen to her. The minister didn't give her any answers; he just embraced her and wept with her. And it seemed to me that Smith was saying that all the theology doesn't really matter. What really matters when these terrible things happen is that we reach out to each other and show compassion and empathy.

Frank Geer: A few days after September 11, I got a call from a reporter named Jane Brody who writes a health column for the *New York Times*. She was writing a story on counseling people affected by the disaster. And she said, "If you could give someone trying to help others traumatized by the disaster one piece of advice, what would it be?" I had to really think for a moment. Then I said to her: "Be a compassionate listener. Listen to somebody when they want to tell their story about where they were, what they felt, who they were with on September 11. Listen in a way that indicates compassion and understanding. The great thing about doing that is that if I do that to you, you're probably going to do that to me." And immediately, Jane Brody starts telling me where she was on September 11 and what she was going through. And when she finished, I said, "I would guess that you feel a little bit better having told me that and having had me listen to it." Then I told her my story. And after talking to her, I remember thinking that the disaster itself had a ripple effect. The pain and the horror and the tragedy of it spread out through the world like the ripples on a pond when a pebble's been thrown in. But the healing travels back the other way, like the same ripples coming back towards the center after they've reached the shore.

II
HELPING A FIREMAN COPE

HELPING A FIREMAN COPE

John Horgan: At what point did theological issues arise either in your own mind as you mulled this over, or in a conversation that you were having with people you were counseling?

Frank Geer: In one sense, theological issues emerged immediately. I like the saying that feelings are the language of the soul. People were feeling so intensely that day that they were involved in soul work almost right from the beginning. The struggle was not about God or about religion as much as it was about why something like this would happen. The encounter that really sticks out for me was with one very young fireman who had hurt his knee pretty badly. I sat down with him and he told me his story. He'd been part of a group of five rescue workers in one of the towers. He started to feel nauseous and the head of his group said, "Get out, we'll be right behind you." So he ran out of the lobby just before the whole building came down. He hurt his knee when the debris surge knocked him down. And then, with death in his eyes, he looked at me and said, "Those other guys in my team didn't make it out." So we sat and talked for the next hour about why some power had singled him out in that fashion. He was thinking, "How could I be so blessed and how could they be so abandoned?"

John Horgan: These are theological questions.

Frank Geer: Yes, but the young fireman wasn't asking himself these questions in abstract metaphysical terms. He was dealing with the questions in his own life, his own reality: "Why was I saved? Why did they all die? What am I going to do with this?"

John Horgan: Did you try to help him reach some sort of understanding?

Frank Geer: I really just wanted him to stay aware of the ambiguity of his situation. On the one hand, as a young guy with a wife and a couple of kids, he was incredibly happy that he had been saved. On the other hand, he was so ripped up by all the other people who had died. What I said basically was: "You're going to have to come up with an answer that will cover not only the blessings you've received, but also the disaster and the pain. And that's not going to be easy."

John Horgan: One of the questions I address in the book I'm writing about spirituality is why God allows horrible things to happen to completely innocent people. I can't accept the idea that there is some kind of divine intelligence underlying the way blessings and suffering are meted out in this world. I would love to believe that there's some higher power out there that cares for humanity, or for me personally. But I just can't reconcile that with the way I see the world working, and especially with an event like the one we're talking about. This young fireman felt sick. That's what saved him. Wasn't it just luck?

Frank Geer: So you would say to that fireman, "Look, this is life. You were lucky and they weren't." And that certainly is an alternative explanation. The meaning he was attributing to what happened that day is what I would characterize as religious, whereas the meaning that you attribute to it is non-religious. You are trying to take his salvation out of the religious realm and make it just another of the vagaries of life, without any deeper meaning assigned to it.

John Horgan: That is how most scientists view life. Most scientists say life as a whole is here not through divine decree, but through some kind of accident. Life is a kind of fluke that emerged from the laws of nature. There was no particular reason for us to be here, and there's no particular reason for us to endure. We might be extinguished any day either because of our own foolishness or because an asteroid strikes the earth. It seems like a pretty bleak world-view, but it accords with the way nature works.

Frank Geer: I can tell you that in no way did that fireman I talked to on September 11 think it all comes down to luck. He had a very strong, clear feeling of having been delivered. He had an incredible gratitude for the force that had saved him. But at the same time, he's saying: "Wait a second. This same power that saved me abandoned my four comrades. Why? If this is a loving God, how can he be so gracious to me and so unresponsive and cruel to them? My wife is home crying tears of joy because she knows I'm alive, and four other wives are home totally despondent, because their husbands died." This kind of raw inconsistency is part of all our lives. Our lives are full of such blessings and, at the same time, instances where we and the people around us seem to be abandoned. One temptation is to seize upon the abandonment and say, "This is the nature of the universe. It's a lonely, cruel, impersonal place governed exclusively by chance." But we also have evidence every day in our lives that that's not true.

John Horgan: How can we prevent that sense of personal salvation or attention from God from mutating into something malignant? That's obviously what happened in the case of the people who hijacked those planes, and that's obviously true of religious fanaticism in general. The beautiful part of religion—the feeling that things will work out for the best, that we're here for a reason, that the universe in some sense cares for us—can become something lethal and evil.

Frank Geer: That's a very good point. In a sense, you're saying there's a similarity in kind between the feelings the firefighter was having on the afternoon of September 11 and the feelings that the hijackers were having on the morning of September 11 before they hit the Towers. Both the firefighter and the hijackers felt blessed, beloved, and chosen by God. And that's a scary thought, because it's saying that religious sensibility can be a source of enormous personal comfort but it can also be a source of intense pain and suffering to others. And, boy, if there's something we've experienced over and over and over again in our culture and our civilization, it's that enduring truth about religion—what can be such a powerful comfort to people can also be an incredibly powerful destructive force.

I believe that two tendencies are probably going to manifest themselves within world religions as a result of September 11. Some people and religious groups will work hard to develop patterns of tolerance and understanding that will limit the destructive effects of religious belief. Others will become even more entrenched in their own faith and even more vindictive toward other groups and other religions. Which of these two tendencies prevails will affect the course of human history. That's why I think this is a pretty critical crossroads in the history of the world.

III
VISITING GROUND ZERO

VISITING GROUND ZERO

Frank Geer: I have a friend here in Garrison, a member of my congregation, who heads a construction company involved in the cleanup of Ground Zero. About a week after September 11, he asked me if I wanted to tour the site. I jumped at the offer, but not without misgivings. In my agitated imagination, I felt as though Vergil was about to take me into the inferno. I was worried that I would be exposed to sights that I just didn't want to see. When I arrived at the site, many of my fears were realized. Part of it was the acrid, electrical, ozone smell. Part of it was the smell of death, from which we are usually insulated in our society. The devastation was so total that it reminded me of pictures of Hiroshima and Nagasaki after we bombed them in World War II. There were mountains of debris, with smoke coming up from fires within them, and firemen and policemen scouring the debris looking for remains of their fallen comrades and other victims. There were huge steel beams twisted like wire and girders sticking into the sides of neighboring buildings forty stories up. But what was even more weird about the Trade Center site was the abruptness of the transition from the center of total devastation to the perimeter of total preservation. Three blocks away you had totally unscathed buildings and newsstands and bagel shops.

Anyway, as I toured the site my mood quickly changed from dismay almost to exhilaration because the people that I met there were so wonderful. They were such professionals and doing such a good job cleaning up. Even though it was a nightmare scenario, these construction guys, policemen, and firemen were systematically cleaning up the mess, recovering the remains, doing everything that needed to be done. And I went away from that visit just incredibly impressed and proud of all of them. And the big thing that was said to me over and over again was, "No one else is going to die." And as far as I know, nobody has, even though that day and for weeks after there were people hanging off steel girders forty stories in the air and others burrowing into void spaces in the smoking rubble—incredibly dangerous things like that.

John Horgan: That's amazing.

Frank Geer: Something else happened that day at the site. I was wearing my clerical collar, and as I was walking around I felt a hand on my shoulder. When I turned around there was this really dusty, tired looking man with all the fireman's gear on:

the hat, the orange coat and the boots, and the radios and equipment. And in the middle of all the fire gear was a clerical collar.

John Horgan: Was he a priest?

Frank Geer: He was a Methodist minister, and one of the chaplains for the Fire Department. He'd been there every day since September 11. He and the other chaplains had been working shifts, 12 hours on, 12 hours off. We had a nice talk. I said to him, "What do you do?" And he said that whenever they find some remains, they all gather around and have a special prayer and bow their heads and have a moment of silence and respect for that person and then they put the remains in one of the bags and wrap them up and send them off to the morgue. He said that such services happened four or five times each shift. Then I said, "In between those times, what do you do?" And he said, "I just hang around and listen to the guys." And you realize that's absolutely key, to have him there to talk to these guys doing the work out there and encountering the horror. They can get some of the pain off their chests before going back in.

About halfway through the tour I thought to myself that I wanted to visit St. Paul's Chapel, an Episcopal church that's 250 years old and is just a block from the World Trade Center site. Although the building was shielded from damage on September 11, it couldn't function as a church because it was in the cordoned zone. The parish instead turned the church into a kind of comfort center for the firemen and policemen and construction people. You could come in and get hot coffee, fresh clothes, a new hat, whatever you needed. And you could pray if you wanted to.

So I asked the group I was with if we could visit St. Paul's Chapel, and they agreed. And when we walked inside the place was humming; it was full of people helping and being helped. But, in spite of all this busyness, we were acutely aware that this is a holy place. So I said, "Let's say a prayer"—and this group of people who'd just toured hell lowered their heads while I said a prayer. I prayed first and foremost for all the people who had died the previous Tuesday. I prayed for their families, and I prayed for the workers who were risking their lives every day at the site. I prayed that God would watch over them and keep them safe. Then I prayed for the five of us who were gathered there with joined hands and asked him to watch over us too.

John Horgan: I know from talking to a couple of the people who were with you that day how moving that moment was.

Frank Geer: Yes. I'm not sure how important religion is to them ordinarily. They may have grown up exposed to the tools of religion and abandoned those tools in their adult lives, probably for very sound reasons. But that day, after that shared experience of touring Ground Zero, it was important for them to be able to pick up those tools again, if only for a minute.

IV
FINDING COMFORT IN NATURE

FINDING COMFORT IN NATURE

John Horgan: I agree that we all have to find ways—or tools, as you call them—to remind ourselves of all that makes life worth living, in spite of all the terrible things that can happen.

Frank Geer: Our tools that day in St. Paul's Chapel were prayers, and the space—the holy space. I'm not saying the tools we had that day were the only tools available. I am saying it's important to know what your tools are and not to forget them because you never know when you're going to need them. On September 11, you and your wife walked up the hill behind your house and looked at the smoke coming from the city. Well, those were your tools.

John Horgan: Yes. In the weeks after September 11, my wife and I spent a lot of time just walking in the woods. It was enormously reassuring to see the birds flying around in the trees oblivious to all this human tragedy unfolding around them. Even though we humans were doing terrible things to each other, nature was going on as always, and that was a big source of comfort for me. But this also fed my atheistic, or agnostic, outlook. I realized that if we destroy ourselves tomorrow…

Frank Geer: …the birds will still be singing in the trees.

John Horgan: That's right. I equate nature with God in this respect. If there is a God, I think he is a very remote God. Maybe he created us, but at this point, we're on our own. And we can't rely on him to save us. The only way we're going to save ourselves is if we abandon our primordial hatreds and conflicts and somehow realize that we'll be saved together or not at all.

Frank Geer: Nature is an incredible source of comfort and support to people who have access to it. I know someone here in town who on the afternoon of September 11 got together with all her friends in her back yard. They formed a circle around a big oak tree in her back yard and held hands and prayed for the people who had died and for the families and for each other. And I mean prayed not in the sense of organized religion, but just getting together to express concern and love and emotion.

Having said that, religion was also an incredible source of comfort for people. Late on the night of September 11, I walked back to my parents' apartment through the streets of Manhattan after a long and trying day at the hospital. Every church, every synagogue, every mosque I passed—I saw that its doors were open, the lights were on, and the clergy and many, many members of the congregation were out on the street and inviting passersby in if they so chose. Not proselytizing; not saying, "You have to come in—we've got the answer." But basically just saying: "If you need help, come in here. We'll do our best. Make yourself at home; you're welcome here."

At my church here in Garrison, for a couple of Sundays after September 11, our services were as full as they ever are on Christmas and Easter. People wanted to be together. If you want to put a religious element to it, they wanted to be together with other human beings and with God. Going to church was a way to activate and amplify their sense of God and make more tangible the spiritual part of their lives—the part that wants to be together with a force that cares about them, that cares for them.

John Horgan: People comforted each other outside of churches, too. My family doesn't belong to a church, but after September 11 we reached out to friends and talked about the experience; and I guess that's what everybody—whether religious or non-religious—was doing in one way or another. I remember in the week after September 11, there was a fundraising barbecue at the school our kids go to. The organizers of it apparently agonized over whether to hold it or not because they worried it might be in bad taste. And it turned out to be wonderful. It was what everybody needed, to get out and talk with other people and share our anxieties and sense of relief.

V
THE SCANDAL OF PARTICULARITY

THE SCANDAL OF PARTICULARITY

John Horgan: Does part of you ever think that everything in life really just comes down to luck?

Frank Geer: No. I was raised in a Christian family. My Mom and Dad took their religion seriously. I could see that it gave them a lot of comfort and strength and courage, and I seem to have absorbed their faith with my mother's milk. From my earliest memory to this day, I have always believed in Christianity. My faith says, "It's not luck. There is a God out there who's watching out for us." Yesterday I was at the hospital with one of my parishioners who's very sick with cancer and is probably going to die soon. One of the nurses in the hospital came and sang her that beautiful hymn that says, "God's eye is on the sparrow, and I know he watches me." And I've always believed that.

Then again, I've had moments when I've wondered.

John Horgan: There is a phrase that theologians sometimes use, called "the scandal of particularity," which refers to the idea that God treats different people differently. This idea is essential to all the world's religions, not just the Western religions but also Buddhism and Hinduism. Karma and reincarnation suggest that there is a supernatural moral order in the Universe: if you act well, you'll be rewarded in your next life. And if Christians behave well, they go to heaven instead of hell. This is the core of religious belief, but it is also a terribly destructive idea. Instead of thinking, "Everything comes down to luck," you think: "God likes me better than you, and so he's treated me better or will treat me better in the future. I'll go to heaven instead of hell." It was a belief like this that led the terrorists to hijack those airliners on September 11. If that young fireman you talked to on September 11 believes God saved him for a purpose, maybe he'll do wonderful things as a result. But that same belief can give rise to terrible consequences, including the terrorist attacks on the World Trade Towers. That's why I have such a hard time with that whole concept.

Frank Geer: On September 11, three thousand people died in an instant; twenty-six thousand people got out safely. Why? It's that reality that forces us to start playing around with answers like the scandal of particularity. I don't want to defend that religious stance; I don't believe that God plays favorites. I'm saying, "If that answer isn't good enough for you, come up with a better one." I said to that young fireman: "You're going to need to find something in your soul that's going to be able to embrace both those realities—your particular salvation and the general horror."

John Horgan: How can religions minimize the adverse effects of this belief that there is a God watching over us? How do you avoid that culminating in a belief that God is on your side and not on someone else's side? This is the belief that leads some quarterback who has just won the Super Bowl to say that he won because he and his teammates all prayed before the game and God listened to their prayers. This is essentially the same kind of thinking that led to the Crusades and the Inquisition and other great evils perpetrated in the name of religion throughout history.

Frank Geer: I'm not in any way denying that a lot of serious damage is done in the name of religion. And most of it is a direct result of that sense that God is watching over me and not these other people. But religion can also give us a healthy sense that we're all in this together. At the end of a football game, you often see a bunch of the players from both teams form a big circle in the middle of the field, and they kneel down and pray together. These guys who've been whacking into each other as hard as they can a minute ago are now holding hands together.

John Horgan: Except if there are Muslims or Jews or atheists on those football teams—they're not part of that prayer circle. If we all believed in the same faith, there wouldn't be any problem. But we all have different faiths. There certainly are common elements in all religions, but for some people the differences are more important than the commonalities, and the differences justify these terrible acts of hatred. Christianity obviously isn't as insistent on its own superiority as it used to be. It's more tolerant of other religions. Certainly there are Christian fanatics, pro-life people who shoot abortion doctors and so forth, but somehow mainstream Christianity has for the most part seemed to move past that fanaticism. I wonder if there's some shift in emphasis that can make a religion less susceptible to fanaticism.

Frank Geer: Since September 11, I have told people who are very enthusiastic and exclusive Christians, "That's not good enough anymore." I talked to one friend who was part of a Christian group that donated food to the people in a village in Afghanistan that had been devastated by shelling and bombing. He and his group are performing a wonderful work of charity, saving hundreds of lives this winter. My friend said to me that he met with a village leader and told him: "I pray for you and your people every day and I especially pray that you will come to know my God. For, if you do, you'll learn that my God loves you, even though you are a Muslim."

And I said, "You have to understand how deeply you insulted that village leader. It's clear that Islam, Christianity, and Judaism are really talking about one and the same God. For you to say, '*My* God loves you,' is like slapping him in the face. And to pray for him to embrace *your* God is another slap in the face. You need to realize that there's already a commonality to what he believes and what you believe."

VI
INCREASING RELIGIOUS TOLERANCE

INCREASING RELIGIOUS TOLERANCE

John Horgan: I find some of the religious rhetoric inspired by September 11 very frightening. When President Bush called the terrorists "evil," he was suggesting that God is on our side in our war against terrorism and not on the side of the terrorists. The terrorists have certainly committed horrible crimes and deserve to be punished, but I think it's wrong for us to see our battle with them in supernatural, religious terms. The terrible irony is that we are succumbing to the very sort of thinking that motivated the terrorists—that "God is on our side."

Frank Geer: One of the questions people have been asking since September 11 is what can we do about this problem of religious intolerance. There was a wonderful man who used to live here in Garrison, named René Dubos. He was a biologist and philosopher who coined the aphorism, "Think globally, act locally." In other words, we may not be able to solve the problem on a universal level, but there are things you can do to solve the problem in your neighborhood and with the people that you know.

What my congregation and I have been dealing with since September 11—and what many religious groups across the world have been dealing with—is increasing the awareness that we have to develop new forms of faith and cooperation and worship. We're not radically changing everything we believe, but changing how we relate to other groups of believers. After September 11, at the church here in Garrison, our adult class spent several weeks studying Islam. We asked questions like, "Is the God that they call Allah the same as our God?" and, "What's the relationship between Jesus and Muhammad?"

We combed local resources—books, tapes, Muslim groups, professors of religion—in our search for answers to these questions. We soon realized that, in order to understand Islam, we had to study Judaism, too. We designed a new curriculum to study the commonalities and divergencies among the world's three great monotheistic religions; and, in particular, how attitudes of intolerance emerge in all three.

Our studies culminated in our holding an interfaith Christmas pageant. I wrote a scene that was acted out by the kids in which a baby born to a Jewish mother and Muslim father is visited on Christmas Eve by a Muslim family, a Jewish family, and a Christian family—who all come to witness the glory of life and pledge themselves to work a little harder to respect that glory. Everybody in the church responded positively, even some people I thought would be the most entrenched in their Christianity. Maybe some people thought our children shouldn't be learning about Islam on Christmas. Maybe they're all feeling that way, and they're just not telling me. But, honestly, I think September 11 was such a powerful event that people are ready for a new reality of tolerance to emerge in their religious lives.

John Horgan: Listening to you talk about teaching the kids in your church about Islam, I couldn't help but think of John Walker Lindh, the young man from California who was fighting with the Taliban when he was captured in Afghanistan. He grew up in a very tolerant, intellectual, liberal home in Marin County, California, center of the New Age, and he seized upon Islam. One reason may be that Islam offered him certainty. That's what a lot of people look for in religion. Religion offers security, an anchor that keeps you grounded. But then that can mutate into absolutism and fanaticism.

Frank Geer: Since September 11, many religious people I've talked to have been very disturbed and shaken by what we're talking about, the potential abuses of religion. They've been thinking about what we can do to draw the line, to keep this aspect of human endeavor from going way overboard and becoming a destructive force. The attitude that makes the most sense to me is one in which the believer says: "This religion—in my case, Christianity—can be extraordinarily comforting and meaningful. I understand that in certain times it is in opposition to other systems of understanding reality, and I'm willing to live with that. I'm committed to Christianity as something that means an awful lot to me. I'm also committed to the idea that it's not the only way of interpreting reality and that I may be wrong."

John Horgan: Do you think the doubt that you just expressed should be a part of any religious tradition?

Frank Geer: After September 11, I'm beginning to think that it ought to be. If we are creatures who can *evolve*, that's the direction we need to evolve towards. We need to recognize that it's okay to passionately believe something and derive meaning and support from it. But we also need to be aware that the passion with which we hold a belief does not justify certainty that our belief is a universal truth which it is a mortal error not to believe. And when I say *evolve*, I'm using scientific rather than religious language. But you can say that that is the direction that God's spirit is pointing us in the twenty-first century. God is leading the human spirit in the direction of understanding each of our world religions as one of many of equal validity. In the wake of September 11, there have been calls by religious leaders everywhere for renewed efforts at mutual understanding and education among the world's religious communions. And, in the spirit of René Dubos, that's what we're doing right here in Garrison. The problem is, how far can we go in doing that?

John Horgan: How tolerant can you be and remain a religion?

Frank Geer: How tolerant can you be before the people in your church start looking for another church, because they say: "My children don't even know about Christianity. I bring them here to Sunday school to learn about Christianity and they're learning about Islam and other faiths." I think that's a real challenge, because it's drastically important to teach both our own faith and tolerance of other faiths. As a person who pretty much has given his life to functioning within the structures of an organized religion, I have been especially gripped since September 11 by the realization that we no longer can afford the luxury of imagining that the communal truth that gives us so much comfort is somehow a universal truth that would or should comfort everybody. That is too risky an opinion to hold, and it leads to fanatics flying planes into the World Trade Center.

John Horgan: How tolerant can you be when intolerant fanatics target you, your family, and your country for destruction? Should you seek vengeance or should you turn the other cheek?

Frank Geer: Forgiveness is an essential part of the Christian faith. It is an aspect of Christianity that makes our religion unique. We are taught to practice radical forgiveness of all transgressors against us under all circumstances. Pope John Paul II visited the man who tried to kill him. He forgave him and tried to help him understand the source and meaning of that forgiveness. Jesus taught us to turn the other cheek and to be ready to forgive without qualification those who hurt us countless times. We believe this teaching comes from God and is a reflection of God's limitless love for us. For Christians, forgiveness of those who planned and carried out the attacks of September 11 is a necessary outcome and proof of who we are and what we believe.

VII
FINDING PATTERNS AND MEANING

FINDING PATTERNS AND MEANING

John Horgan: What do you think is the core tenet of all religions?

Frank Geer: What makes a religion a religion is that very real sense that there is some divine hand at work in our lives. If you start to imagine that's not true, then you're leaving religion behind. But that sensibility of some divine hand at work is very common in our culture. We can talk about being a secular culture; we can talk about being a society that has moved away from religion. But you go to an Alcoholics Anonymous meeting, you read the media and many cultural commentaries, and what they say, over and over again, is that—even though the forms of religion may be decaying and the practice of religion may be declining—most people still feel that a divine hand is somehow at work in the universe, in human history, and in their personal lives.

John Horgan: Science has addressed this almost universal intuition that humans have had that there's a divine intelligence behind things. Psychology and cognitive science have shown that our brains are enormously sensitive machines for finding cause-and-effect relationships, or patterns, in nature. Science itself is one product of our phenomenal ability to look at the apparently random flux of nature and extract meaningful patterns from it. Science is a method of finding patterns that actually exist. For as long as we've existed, humans have had a tendency to find human patterns, anthropomorphic patterns, in nature.

Religion is a product of that tendency. We perceive comets or storms or droughts as a message for us from some supernatural intelligence, from God. I see that as an example of our pattern-detection mechanism perceiving patterns that don't really exist. What science tells us is that this is a vast, strange, wild, inhuman universe with black holes and colliding galaxies, and for some strange reason, we just happened to pop up in this one little corner. When you see things from this cosmic perspective, it's very hard to believe that the whole universe was created for our benefit. That's where science and religion are most at odds.

Frank Geer: In a sense you're suggesting that the scientific approach—and maybe the more useful approach—would be to observe patterns in nature but stop short of assigning meaning to them, because that's where we start to get in trouble. But I guess my experience of the human condition is that it's very hard to not cross that bridge—to absorb things and not assign meaning to them. It's very difficult and unusual for people to do that.

And a good example is the sort of trauma that people had after September 11. There were hundreds of thousands of people who weren't as directly as involved in the World Trade Center catastrophe as the fireman we talked about earlier, but who were still personally affected by its consequences. Maybe they worked in the neighborhood and had to evacuate; maybe they had a friend who was killed; maybe they watched the Towers collapse from their roof in Brooklyn or from the New Jersey waterfront; maybe they just watched the disaster footage play over and over again on television. In counseling, I often hear such people say: "I can't sleep at night. I'm worried about my children. I'm afraid to go into New York."

When we start to unpack their fears and anxieties, often stories from earlier in their life will start to come back. We'll hear about when grandma died, twenty years ago; and about when Kennedy got shot; and about the time that they were out on the ocean in a boat and the boat broke down and they thought that they might die. And you realize that the meaning that they are associating with September 11 is being fed and amplified by all these past patterns. I guess what I'm saying is that human beings are going to search for meaning no matter what. Religious systems help provide people with common, stress-tested, agreed-upon patterns—as opposed to purely particular patterns improvised in the heat of the moment—that give meaning to traumatic experiences and blunt their emotional impact.

John Horgan: I agree that we're all compelled to find meaning. Not even the most atheistic, nihilistic, materialistic scientist—somebody like the evolutionary biologist Richard Dawkins—can live without meaning. We're compelled to find meaning, in the same way we have to breathe. But it seems to me that it's possible to create personal meaning. Religion takes the personal quest for meaning—your own attempt to find things that matter to you and that you love and can cherish—and makes it transcendent and universal. Religion insists that there are universal meanings and values. I can understand the appeal of that impulse, because it broadens your meaning and connects you to other people and even the entire universe, but that impulse can go wrong in lots of ways.

Frank Geer: Religion does make meaning more communal. It takes what happens at an individual level and pushes it in the direction of being a communal experience. There's a certain comfort in that. If my experience is communal, I'm not out there all by myself. My experience is not totally idiosyncratic, because there are other people who have felt the same way and interpreted those feelings the same way. But you're right that the next step that religion so often takes is generalizing what is a vital communal experience into a prescriptive universal experience, and that's where so many of the problems come from.

John Horgan: Yes, and this universal meaning somehow ossifies into dogma. One question that I've asked a lot of religious scholars is why art can't serve the same purpose that religion serves. And by art I mean not just graphic art but also poetry and literature and music—all forms of artistic expression. They help us find meaning and share meaning. But art says: "This is the way things could be;" or, "Try looking at things this way;" or, "Here's an experience that someone else has had that maybe you have had, and here's a possible meaning of that experience." But art doesn't ossify into truth or dogma the way that religion so often does. Religion obviously has a very powerful artistic expression, but at some point religion goes beyond art and says not, "This is how things could be," but: "This is how things are. This is what you should believe."

VIII

SODOM AND GOMORRAH
AND THE
TWIN TOWERS

SODOM AND GOMORRAH
AND THE
TWIN TOWERS

Frank Geer: One answer to your question as to why we need religions is that there's a practical, structural side to our search for meaning that needs to be organized and tended to. That fireman I counseled on September 11 no doubt went in the weeks that followed to the funerals for his four fallen teammates and those rituals probably helped him to deal with what had happened to him. He could have contacted the four surviving spouses of the guys that died and talked about what their last moments were like. Maybe he did—but making conversation about circumstances of death and implications of loss can be unbearably painful when bereavement is fresh. By going to the funerals, the young fireman could connect to the bereaved families of his fallen comrades at a bearable remove. The forms of religion provided him a safe zone in which to share his grief and respect with the widows and families.

John Horgan: I recently went to the funeral of one of my oldest friends, someone I've known since high school. He was my age, 48, with two young kids, a big, strong guy who was suddenly stricken with cancer and died. I'd never felt the value of religion more than during his funeral service, which was in a Methodist church. The religion provided a framework and a ritual for our grieving. But what really made the funeral profound and moving was the people there, sharing their grief and consoling each other and telling stories about Charlie. And so I still ended up thinking, "Why can't we have that sharing process without the religious framework?"

Frank Geer: Well, in addition to providing us with rituals that give structure to our search for meaning, religious texts such as the Bible and the Koran can also help us reconcile the two antagonistic realities of life: the good and the bad. Great minds and souls have been working on this problem for over two thousand years, and it'd be a little arrogant for me to imagine that I've got to start all over again and that I can't take advantage of their insights. I can look in the Bible and read a story written twenty-five hundred years ago that's dealing with exactly the same issues we all dealt with after September 11. A week after the attack, I stood on a parapet looking at the remains of the Twin Towers, and I thought of the scene in the Hebrew Bible where Abraham is standing on the hillside overlooking Sodom and Gomorrah. Where these two great cities used to be, he sees nothing but smoke and ashes. That is what I saw at Ground Zero.

John Horgan: But that's the kind of story that gives religion and God a bad name. Sodom and Gomorrah were destroyed by God because he was angry with the behavior of their inhabitants. And, of course, after September 11, you had the Christian leaders Jerry Falwell and Pat Robertson suggesting that, in the same way, God might have destroyed the people in the World Trade Towers as punishment for the sins of certain people in the United States. These ideas are abhorrent to me.

Frank Geer: In the Book of Genesis there are actually two stories about Sodom and Gomorrah. One story tells how the Lord rained down brimstone and fire and slew all the inhabitants of Sodom and Gomorrah, apart from Lot, his wife, and their two daughters, who were allowed to escape. Right before this story is another story in which God tells Abraham he is going to destroy Sodom and Gomorrah because they're so wicked. Abraham then bargains with God, flattering his divine sense of the injustice of destroying the righteous along with the wicked. The story ends with God's conceding that he will not destroy Sodom and Gomorrah if only ten righteous inhabitants can be found in them.

Generally, these two stories are viewed as sequential: ten righteous people could not be found, so the cities were destroyed. But a more nuanced interpretation is that two alternative stories are preserved here side by side in the Book of Genesis because the Judeo-Christian tradition is subtle enough to accommodate the simultaneous possibility of opposite divine verdicts. The tradition says, "You decide which makes more sense—a world where everybody gets destroyed because some people are wicked; or a world where everybody gets saved because some people are good." And you learn a lot about churches and synagogues and mosques by observing which story they tend to home in on: the story of Abraham's compassion or the story of brimstone and fire.

John Horgan: Religion can give us an optimism and faith that things will turn out all right, which obviously have practical value in getting us through difficult times. Religion also teaches us to have compassion for each other. But I don't see why we can't have those values without the superstructure of religion, which causes so much misunderstanding and conflict between us. All religions teach that we should care for each other, but they do it in a complicated way that invokes supernatural principles. Common sense tells us that the only way we're all going to survive in this world is if we at least tolerate and at best really care for each other. As soon as you invoke God, you get these disagreements about what God really wants. Does God want us to be compassionate as Abraham was when he asked God to spare Sodom and Gomorrah? Or does God want us to help him destroy those wicked cities?

IX

APOCALYPTIC FEARS AND FORETELLINGS

APOCALYPTIC FEARS AND FORETELLINGS

John Horgan: I went down to the Twin Towers site recently and, reading all the posters pinned to the barricades around the site, I was struck by how many insisted that September 11 is the beginning of the end of the world as foretold in Revelation or Ezekiel or Nostradamus or some other prophetic text. I've even heard this kind of apocalyptic rhetoric from friends who I thought were quite rational and areligious.

Frank Geer: The apocalyptic thinking inspired by September 11 may not have anything to do with religion. It has to do with human emotions. At our church here we have a group of junior high school kids that meets every Sunday. On the Sunday after September 11, the kids all talked about how frightened they had been that Tuesday morning. One thought the world was going to end; another thought World War III had started; and another one worried that Indian Point, the nuclear power plant near us, had melted down and the radiation was going to kill her. Similarly, at the hospital on September 11, people were running up to the emergency room entrance with all kinds of stories: "The air has been poisoned! We're all going to die!" "Those planes were filled with anthrax! The whole city has been contaminated!" Apocalyptic fears and rumors like these naturally emerge when a real crisis is unfolding and not yet understood. And they naturally recede as the crisis abates.

John Horgan: But some religious doctrines seem to encourage the idea of a grand apocalyptic ending, hopefully a happy ending. To me, the idea of a happy ending is a contradiction in terms. I don't see the Last Judgment as such a happy ending. Personally, I prefer theologies that promise us eternal life. Hinduism is one example, because it describes existence as an eternal cycle of death and rebirth.

Frank Geer: You could certainly see apocalyptic concerns reflected in the ways that people talked about September 11. In those first few days, there were all sorts of ways that people described the site at the World Trade Center. Then somebody said, "Ground Zero;" and, pretty soon, maybe a week later, everybody was referring to the site as *Ground Zero*. At first that name's military connotation really bothered me, because the term *Ground Zero* refers to a bombsight. When you look through a bombsight, there are two cross hairs, and the numbers go plus and minus in one direction and plus and minus in the other direction. And basically the bomb is going to hit where the two cross hairs meet, at zero. In my life, when people refer to *Ground*

Zero they're usually talking about a nuclear attack. They'd say, "If you're this far from Ground Zero, you have a zero percent chance of surviving; and if you're this far from Ground Zero, you have a twenty-five percent chance of surviving." *Ground Zero* evokes the primal fear of my generation—the fear that we would all be obliterated in a nuclear Armageddon. So it was very disquieting to me that the World Trade Center site was called Ground Zero. It is not just a neutral term; it is freighted with an apocalyptic connotation of universal destruction.

Then I took that tour of the site a week after the attacks, and there was a point where I thought to myself, "This *is* Ground Zero." And what it meant to me was that this is the point from which we have to start to rebuild. We are down to nothing as a society, as a civilization, and as a species when one group of human beings can do this to another group of human beings in the name of God. We have to come together to create something of true and lasting value, and we're starting from scratch. And by implication I'm saying: religion is starting from scratch, because, by allowing us to get to this point, religion has failed us. Science is starting from scratch, too, because, by allowing us to get to this point, science has failed us. In politics we're starting from scratch. In economics we're starting from scratch. I know this is an exaggeration; it's not entirely true. But that's the powerful feeling that I had then.

Maybe that's an apocalyptic feeling, but to me it felt not like an end but a beginning, or an end and a beginning. And actually, in the context of our discussion about patterns, the pattern of endings as beginnings, destruction as rebirth, is part of many religious traditions. Certainly it's part of the Hindu religious traditions, as you pointed out. And it's a very real part of the Christian story of the resurrection of Christ.

John Horgan: But Christianity also has the notion of a final End Time, the Last Judgment, the end of death and rebirth.

Frank Geer: We Christians have to be very careful about these notions. The early Christians, notably the apostle Paul, regarded Jesus' conquest of death in his resurrection as the sole foundation of their faith, being the means of the Christian believer's personal redemption and rebirth into eternal life. The full articulation of Christian apocalyptic ideas came two centuries after Paul, in such writings as the Book of Revelation. It's clear from the Gospels that Jesus did have extreme visions and that his view of the world was to some extent apocalyptic. He had an acute sense that cosmically significant events were unfolding through him that would be brought to a dramatic supernatural conclusion in the future. But Jesus' views were not dogmatized, and the elaborate visionary formulations of the Last Days and Second Coming were later accretions. The historical and doctrinal core of the Christian faith is the resurrection and teachings of Jesus—not apocalyptic dogma.

X
THE RESURRECTION AND OTHER MIRACLES

THE RESURRECTION AND OTHER MIRACLES

John Horgan: So you can be a good Christian without believing in the Last Judgment, the Apocalypse, the End Time? That's not essential to Christianity?

Frank Geer: No. There is one story that is the foundation of the entire Christian faith, and that is the story of an itinerant preacher from Galilee, who came to Jerusalem to witness an idea. It was the idea of an abundant world. It was the idea of a faith that was based on love. It was the idea of the Kingdom of God, which is a dramatic reality beyond the reality we encounter and live in during the course of our day-to-day lives. The Kingdom of God is an immanent end time when the accounts of the human heart will be drawn up and washed clean; when old ways and laws will shut down and new opportunities and a new freedom will arise.

This preacher came to Jerusalem to reveal the Kingdom of God to the people, and as a result he was arrested, he was humiliated, he was condemned by the secular authorities at the behest of the religious authorities. All his friends and supporters abandoned him. He was taken to a hilltop and nailed to a cross and subjected to the most brutal sort of death that people in those days could imagine. The only people who didn't abandon him were the women who were part of his group. The women stuck with him; the men all ran away. He died; he was buried; and, three days later, he arose from the dead.

That's the story upon which Christianity is based. Over the centuries, all sorts of interpretation and elaboration have been overlaid on that original story. Connections have been made with the parent source, the Judaic tradition. Patterns from various contemporary religions and cults have been tied in with that story. But the Gospel story of the carpenter from Galilee is the irreducible center of everything else.

John Horgan: Do you believe that Jesus was just a man, who happened to have an amazing ability to inspire people and to help them see reality in fresh ways? Or do you believe that Jesus was different than the rest of us in the sense of having supernatural powers, of being singled out by God?

Frank Geer: What I believe and what Christianity teaches are close to the same. Jesus was certainly just a man, and he certainly also had God's power in him and was one and the same with God. And Jesus' power is not just something that functioned in a then-and-there way when he walked through Palestine with his disciples. It functions just as vitally in a here-and-now way in the lives of his followers today. And this very brief articulation of faith is the essential credo of Christianity: Jesus was totally a man; he is God; and he is just as real and powerful and present to his followers now as he was to those who followed him when he lived as a man.

John Horgan: Let me see if I can distinguish our views in another way. Do you believe in miracles? The resurrection, interpreted as a literal event, would be a miracle.

Frank Geer: Yes. The resurrection is the miracle upon which Christianity is based. The great early Christian theologians like Paul said, "Without the resurrection, this is nothing. I don't preach Christ crucified. I preach Christ resurrected." I think that all the other miracle stories—turning water into wine, the virgin birth, raising Lazarus from the dead, and everything else—all point to that resurrection. In a sense, they're all part of a process, a story that's saying: "Here's somebody who can do these sort of things early on in his life. So wouldn't it make sense that he could also be resurrected from the dead?" The stories show that this is someone around whom the miraculous seems to coalesce. And that's to prepare us for the point of the story when the resurrection occurs.

John Horgan: I guess this is where I'm really a non-believer. It gets back to the scandal of particularity. You're suggesting that these miracles associated with Jesus, especially the resurrection, happened because God suspended the laws of nature for him. God treated Jesus differently. I just don't like this notion that God singles out certain people—like Jesus or Muhammad or Buddha or Moses—for special treatment and gives them supernatural powers but not the rest of us. I like it when religions tell us that we're all equal in the eyes of God, including Jesus. I see Jesus as a great leader with inspirational ideas, but not as someone with supernatural powers.

Frank Geer: As you look back on September 11, did you experience in any way the miraculous at work on that day?

John Horgan: I experience the miraculous all the time in the following way. A lot of people agonize over why bad things happen to them, and they ask, "Why me?" My problem is the opposite. My life has been so wonderful that I think, "Why me?" I wonder why I was so lucky rather than unlucky. That's something I felt on September 11 very powerfully. To me, that event demonstrated the randomness of nature, and the violence of nature, and the violence of humanity, because we're part of nature. We were born with our capacity for violence. But the worse things are, the more I sense the miraculousness of all that's good in life. The contrast becomes so extreme that it's almost unbearable for me. At moments like that, I come closest to thinking there must be some sort of plan to existence, even though it's completely inscrutable, because there's so much that's right with the world; the world is so beautiful.

On September 11, after my wife and I walked to the top of that hill and saw the smoke coming up from New York City, we walked back to our house and the birds were singing and the clouds were sailing overhead and everything was so bright and sparkly that it was almost too much to bear. What I sensed at that moment—and this is as spiritual as I get—was that life is a miracle. It's a completely mysterious miracle, unexplainable by any scientific theory or any theology. I am so grateful to be alive. I just don't know who to be grateful to. I want to be grateful to somebody or something for all the blessings that I have. But if there is some God who deserves thanks for all our blessings, then he also deserves blame for what happened on September 11, and for all the suffering in the world.

Frank Geer: You're saying you did experience the miraculous on September 11. You experienced it in a very profound and personal way.

John Horgan: The feeling I had was really a kind of wonder mixed with awe. I think that this is one area where religion and science converge. Although not all scientists would agree with me on this, I believe that science has proven that our existence is a miracle. Science has no idea why the Big Bang occurred. It has no idea why the universe takes this form rather than an infinite number of other possible forms. There is no reasonable explanation for why life emerged here on earth. There is nothing in the laws of physics or chemistry that suggests that life had to occur. Once life got started, it could have gone in an infinite number of directions, including being extinguished. And yet, somehow, life produced these sentient creatures who can agonize over their existence and ponder their origins. To the extent that we recognize our miraculousness, we should cherish every single moment that we have here on earth.

Frank Geer: Based on people I've talked to since September 11, you're not alone in how you felt that day. People felt, along with the horror, this incredible sense of gratitude, of blessing, bordering on the miraculous. I remember watching on television when the second plane flew right into the South Tower. There was a huge explosion of aviation fuel, and I remember thinking to myself, "How in the world are those two buildings still standing?" I've been in the World Trade Center often, and I thought there is no way those buildings are still standing. For me, it was a miracle that those buildings stood up as long as they did, long enough for most of the people in them to escape with their lives. I've got a hyperactive imagination, and I could almost see God's hands holding up those buildings to allow all those people to get out. And then I could see God letting go and letting those buildings fall down. What's funny now is reading all the scientific explanations of what happened to the buildings. They've done a lot of work on the structural aspects of the steel and the poured concrete and so forth. So what I experienced as a miracle is now being explained scientifically and demythologized. But that day it felt like a miracle to me.

But as I was celebrating the miracle of God holding up those buildings as most of the people got out, I was also struggling with the reality that thousands of people were dead or dying on the upper floors. I was also struggling with the reality of the people who were on the planes. What if you were sitting in the back of the plane in Row 34 looking out the window and seeing the Trade Center come at you at six hundred miles an hour? What is your relationship with God then? Where is the miracle for you?

So here's the great ambiguity again. We need to have a consciousness that's able to encompass this ambiguity—whether it's a religious consciousness or a scientific consciousness or a social and political consciousness.

XI
WHEN HEALING IS DIFFICULT

WHEN HEALING IS DIFFICULT

John Horgan: Have you seen any people who are still so traumatized by September 11 that they're not getting on with their lives and it's difficult for them to function?

Frank Geer: My sense is that enormous healing is taking place and that, by and large, we're all doing much better. About two months after the attacks, after Thanksgiving, I asked the junior high school kids who meet at our church on Sunday how they were doing. These were the same young people I talked to on the Sunday morning after September 11, you will remember. And, basically, they all said, "Quit worrying, Reverend Geer! We're fine!"—and I believed them. I think an awful lot of people are in that place right now; day by day, they're doing better and better. But my sense is that there are some people for whom this has been so difficult that they're still struggling. As a society and as part of any religious group, we must make sure that those people don't get left behind.

John Horgan: How often have you encountered rage or anger among people that you talked to on September 11 or afterwards?

Frank Geer: In New York City on September 11, I encountered pain and confusion and fear. It seemed to me that the more directly involved people were in the actual disaster—whether they were in New York that day or part of the cleanup, or whether they were people who knew someone who died—the more they were gripped by fear and by pain. The people who were less directly involved were more liable to get angry; because for them it was a sense that "something terrible has happened to the collective 'us' and it really makes me angry." I think that the people who were directly involved are getting angry now, down the road. Anger is an inevitable part of the healing process, but I think immediately after September 11 it was crowded out in those most directly affected by pain and fear and sadness. But, when the anger does come into us, we have to be very watchful how we respond to it.

In my sermon on the Sunday after the attacks, I tried to touch on many of the matters pressing so heavily on our hearts; but, in the end, I focused on forgiveness. I said that the attacks had blown a great hole in our souls. Because human nature abhors a vacuum, many passions would rush in to try to fill that hole. Love, mercy, and forgiveness would rush in—but so too would hatred, anger, and revenge. I finished my sermon that morning by warning the congregation to be very careful about what they chose to let into that hole in the weeks and months to come, because they would be stuck with whatever they let in for a very long time. And I urged them, in the name of Christ, to choose love.

John Horgan: At what point do you see these powerful emotional reactions as requiring some sort of psychotherapeutic attention rather than being a natural response to trauma?

Frank Geer: Most mental health or religious organizations can provide that information to you. A number of special brochures and guidebooks have been prepared to help professionals and the general public to recognize post-traumatic stress.

The reality is that New York City and the surrounding region has been grieving since September 11. Although the intensity lessens as you get farther and farther away from New York City, people across the country are going through the same process. Grieving is painful and hard work, but most of us go through it and we start healing and we get better and we come out the other side. But, for whatever reason, there are certain people who don't go through it as smoothly as others, and they're the ones who really do need therapeutic help, which helps them identify and realize why it is that they're not working through the grieving process. It's important to get those people the help they need, because the problems just amplify over time if they're not addressed.

The emergence of certain novelties in an individual's behavior after September 11—such as sleeping disorders, rages, chronic fatigue, fretfulness, reluctance to go out into public places—may signal problems requiring clinical intervention. I would recommend that family, friends, teachers, clergy and health professionals all be on the lookout for people who need help. Certainly help is there for everybody who needs it, because our governments, health organizations, and religious agencies have been making concerted efforts since September 11 to provide adequate mental health resources to meet the public need.

John Horgan: Do you see any general differences in the way that people who have faith react to traumatic events compared to non-believers?

Frank Geer: Not really. It's the same healing process for all of us. For a lot of people, what happened on September 11 brought back vivid memories of earlier traumas—whether collective traumas, such as the day JFK was shot or the day the space shuttle blew up; or private traumas, such as a car accident or the untimely death of a loved one. What was sort of spooky for me was realizing that for my children—your children—September 11 is going to be what they remember twenty years from now when a traumatic event happens. And you get this sense that there's a great underground river of emotional reality that connects us with the past, present and future; and very often I feel that when people are having a hard time dealing with their grief, it's because there's unfinished business that's welling up from this underground river. And I don't think being religious or not being religious has much influence on the hidden channels by which memory invades the grieving process.

John Horgan: Have you seen any significant differences in how people from different age groups responded to September 11?

Frank Geer: For older people, September 11 rekindled memories of other traumatic events. It's like a glass of water with flaky particulate matter in it. Over the years, that stuff has sunk to the bottom so that the liquid is pretty clear, but then September11 comes along and stirs everything up. We find we're having to sort out painful memories that we thought we had laid to rest long ago.

On the brighter side, those of us who are older, like me—I'm 53—life's kicked us around. Experience may help us get on with our lives more quickly and easily than younger people can. Memories of terrible things that have happened in the past can give our older heads some perspective. You don't think, "How can people be so horrible to one another?" because you've seen it over and over in your life.

For a lot of young people, and particularly people in their teens and twenties, this was an incredibly powerful and graphic experience of the horror of life that they'd never experienced before. Before, they may have thought life was just something to enjoy; the bumps in the road are going to be minor and few and far between. So for some young people, September 11 was like hitting a brick wall. It's harder for them to come to terms with it because it was so unexpected and totally unlike anything they'd ever encountered before. I've tried to get them to realize that if it takes them six months or a year or ten years to get over this, that's okay because they really did get walloped. If they ask me how I can get over it, I say, "I've been walloped a few times before, and I've gotten accustomed to getting up and brushing myself off and getting on the best I can."

John Horgan: You and I, when we were growing up, had to face this possibility that the entire world might be destroyed by nuclear war. Do any of these kids have that kind of fear?

Frank Geer: I think that's a generational difference. Worrying about nuclear war was a profound part of our youth. People who are in their teens now have come to consciousness since the fall of the Soviet Union and the end of the Cold War, so they don't have that same primal fear. We older people grew up expecting an apocalyptic event. When the catastrophic but less-than-apocalyptic event occurred on September 11, none of us welcomed it, but we were more prepared for it than the young people.

John Horgan: After the Cold War ended, I really stopped worrying about nuclear war. Then on September 11 I realized that there are people out there who, if they have nuclear weapons, won't hesitate to use them against us. I suddenly felt so sorry that my children will have to grow up fearing this terrible possibility that I thought we'd passed beyond.

Frank Geer: A real difference between you and your children is that you have that memory to be revived. They didn't even have the memory, so for them it's all new territory.

John Horgan: Some of this is new territory for me, too. Just after September 11 there was a report on *60 Minutes* about how officials are worried about terrorists flying an airliner into Indian Point, the nuclear power plant just south of us. We've always had evacuation plans in case there was an accident at Indian Point that released radioactivity, but I don't think anyone ever took those evacuation plans very seriously until now.

Frank Geer: For some really young children, this will be the first trauma of their lives, which will be reawakened in their memories at numerous times for the rest of their lives. Even toddlers too young to fathom the events shown on television absorbed some of the emotional distress from their parents' reactions.

John Horgan: Have you seen any sign that people from different socioeconomic backgrounds have responded differently to September 11?

Frank Geer: My sense was that the attack was a great equalizer on that day. At the hospital where I work, the staff runs the full socioeconomic gamut, as in any large institution. Yet, on September 11, everybody at the hospital pulled together as never before. We had an impromptu chapel service late in the morning, and hospital staff regardless of position were standing side by side holding each others' hands in prayer and embracing one another in tears. All differences and reserve fell away in a community of grief.

Three days later we had another service, this time called and orchestrated by the administrative and medical leadership of the hospital. Even though this was not a spontaneous gathering, it still became another occasion for spontaneous outpouring of common grief. Right after the president of the hospital gave his speech, a janitor stood up uninvited and sang an amazingly affecting rendition of the spiritual, *It Is Well with My Soul*. By the time the last note of the song died away, everybody in the chapel had broken down again as they had on September 11, crying and hugging their neighbors.

John Horgan: A number of people have commented that after September 11 New York City has never been so socially or racially unified.

Frank Geer: Yes. There is an alcohol rehabilitation program at St. Luke's Hospital, and twice a week the other chaplain or I would lead a one-hour class on religion for people in the program. It was a wonderful thing to be part of, but there were days when you'd feel a lot of tension in the room, stemming from the socioeconomic and racial diversity of the group. There were Hispanic people, black people, white people, poor people, and well-to-do people. There was always a tension or edge to the group's interactions that I didn't really understand but was certainly aware of.

But when I met with this group two days after September11, everybody seemed totally together for the first time; there was none of that usual tension. Everyone wanted to know what the day had been like at the hospital. They wanted to hear the stories about the fireman and the others I had talked to, and they were very interested in how I had responded from a religious point of view. This group included Jews, Muslims, Christians, and atheists, about forty people in all, but there was a real sense of everybody all at once going in the same direction.

One member told the group: "I've had a lot of chances to get sober and to create a life for myself, and I've blown them all. But I'm not going blow this one, because those people down at the Trade Center on Tuesday—none of them got another chance. And that made me realize what a gift this chance is for me." You could have heard a pin drop when he said that, because that's the way the other people felt as well. I can't tell you how many people in that group stayed sober. But I can assure you that a lot of people in that group took what he said very seriously and, I would guess, still are taking it very seriously.

XII

WHERE WAS GOD ON SEPTEMBER 11?

WHERE WAS GOD ON SEPTEMBER 11?

John Horgan: There must have been some people you counseled on September 11 or afterwards who asked you in one form or another: "Where was God on September 11?"

Frank Geer: Some people I've counseled since September 11 felt that what happened to them that day was part of a chain of events in which God let them down. What they were saying was, "Why is it I'm abandoned? Why am I always left out in the cold?" And I don't say to them, "Here's how God didn't let you down on September 11." What I say is, "You really need to look at your whole relationship with God. You need to realize that there is a hole there. Let's work on how to adjust your sense of your relationship with God to plug that hole."

So if someone says to me, "Where was God on September 11?" the first thing I'm going to say is, "What do you think?" If they say, "I really don't know," I'll say, "Let's play around with some of the possibilities. Do you think God was driving the plane?" "Oh no, of course not. That was a terribly destructive and evil thing. Whoever was flying the plane was an agent of the devil." "Well, do you think God was with the fireman, the policeman helping the people escape from the building?" "Yeah, that sounds really good. God is there to save us and to help us, saying, 'Keep it going, keep it going.'"

One of my favorite stories that I heard on September 11 was that in a stairwell of one of the towers, thousands of people were surging down the stairs to escape from the building. But on one of the landings—the 32nd or 33rd floor—a woman was in a wheelchair, watching all these people stream by her, realizing that if she pushes out into the flow of traffic in her wheelchair, she's going to clog the whole evacuation and might very well cost hundreds of people their lives. But, at the same time, she realizes she's more and more at risk. By not making the selfish choice, she really is putting herself in mortal danger.

What happened was that one of the people coming down the stairs stopped dead in his tracks. He was an investment banker or someone like that, a pretty big guy. He saw this woman in the wheelchair and immediately understood what was going on and he said, "Come on, honey, you're coming with me"—and he picked her up and swung her over his shoulder and carried her down the thirty flights of stairs on his shoulder, out the lobby, and across to one of the ambulances where she could be taken care of.

When I heard that story, I thought of the parable about the Good Samaritan. Remember, the man is lying there by the side of the road, beaten up and left for dead. And first the priest goes by and leaves him alone. Then the lawyer goes by and leaves him alone. And probably even the scientist would have gone by and left him alone. And it's the sinner, the Samaritan—one of the pariahs of first-century Palestine—who stops and picks the man up and saves his life. One way to read that story is to put yourself in the position of that guy lying on the side of the road and imagine what you would have felt, what sort of questions would have gone through your mind. And that's exactly what that woman was probably feeling as she watched hundreds of people streaming by on the stairwell: "Where's God?" And all of a sudden, this guy picks her up.

So that's one possibility: God was in the being of the investment banker who carried her down the stairs. For people I've counseled, the idea that God was working through the rescue workers, the firemen and policemen, is a very powerful image. I think that's one reason we make such heroes of them, aside from the fact that what they did was patently heroic; people sense that if there was divine salvation at work in that moment, it was in the effort and the presence of the rescue workers. So we can see God's presence at work in the ways that people dealt with this terrible event, the ways that people were delivered from it. But in a way this answer is a cop-out, because it still doesn't answer the larger question: "Why did this happen? In what ways was God implicated in this event as a whole?"

John Horgan: You're bringing up the problem of evil, which is the age-old theological riddle: If God is all-powerful and loves us, then why do such awful things happen to us? Awful things don't just happen to awful people. They happen to totally innocent people. Children who get cancer would be the most obvious example— that's very hard to reconcile with a loving God.

One answer I've heard is that evil gives us an opportunity for learning. We gain something, we grow and become stronger, by suffering, by being exposed to anguish. But then that's saying that six million Jews died in the Holocaust so the rest of us could have a growth experience. There's something perverse about all the attempts to justify evil or reconcile it with this notion of an all-powerful, loving God. And it seems to me that you can't say God was just in the hearts of the firemen or the investment banker, the Good Samaritan who saved the woman; because God is everywhere—or at least that's what I was told in catechism when I was a kid being raised as a Catholic. So God had to be also operating through those terrorists on September 11.

Frank Geer: In small doses, the religious point of view does a lot of good. But when it's taken to extremes, it can be an enormous force for destruction and evil. We can ask, "Where was God on September 11?" And we can get small answers that are very satisfactory: God was in the heroic actions of the firemen and the policemen; God was in the Good Samaritan.

After September 11, there were hundreds of stories of people reaching out to one another. One of the things that has been said to me over and over again about that day by people who were directly involved is, "I have never experienced in my life as powerfully the goodness of other people, of complete strangers, as I did on that day." People were running along the street with fire and jet fuel and debris falling down and someone reaches out and grabs them and pulls them into a storefront or into a shop and says, "Don't be out there. You'll be safer in here." And then when things start to quiet down, they run out together. Now this is someone they didn't know. Someone who just saw another human being and said, "Okay, I have to reach out and grab them and save them."

Good Samaritan activity was epidemic that day. So here are little things, and you can say that God was in the little things. But that doesn't explain the big reality. The big reality is that this incredible evil was done, and God must have had a hand in that whole thing. You could say that if religion doesn't encompass and explain that entire reality and reconcile it with our concept of God, then it's somehow inadequate. But when religion does attempt to explain everything and is taken to universal extremes, it can become a destructive force.

John Horgan: So do you think we should resist trying to find answers to the question of where God was on September 11, and how God could allow this episode to occur? Are you suggesting that we should stop short of trying to come up with an ultimate answer to that question?

Frank Geer: I imagine that it would be totally contrary to human nature not to look for an answer. And it does not seem to be a smart thing to give people counsel totally contrary to human nature.

John Horgan: So Frank, how do you, personally, answer the question: "Where was God on September 11?"

Frank Geer: You really want to know how I respond to the problem of evil?

John Horgan: Right.

Frank Geer: You mentioned the idea that God is teaching us a lesson. You can articulate that in a way that is less cruel and more humane than your characterization, although it's still not entirely satisfactory. God has a plan, and the plan is working itself out. But sometimes things happen that are so terrible and so destructive that we totally lose sight of the plan. It goes back to the part of us that's looking for patterns. Sometimes it's easy to recognize the pattern, but other times we totally lose track of it. It's like being out in the woods and getting totally lost. All the landmarks that you count on to get home and to find safety are gone, and you just don't know where you are. Religion tells us that even when you feel that way, the plan is still in effect, and the plan is working itself out.

One wonderful example of that in the Hebrew Bible is the story of Joseph. His envious brothers beat him up and throw him in a pit and sell him as a slave to be carried off to Egypt. He has all these awful adventures; he's thrown in prison and accused of all sorts of terrible crimes. But eventually, thirteen years later, he's Pharaoh's right-hand man. And his father and brothers come to Egypt and are starving to death and he's in the position to give them grain to keep them alive. This is the story of a man whose life seems to go totally off track and yet he ends up becoming the person who is essential to the survival of his family and the preservation of Israel.

This is a powerful story of how God can work in unexpected ways. I like to think about God's work as the operation of inscrutable providence rather than the way you characterized it earlier—that God is teaching us an object lesson. But if there is a lesson in the story of Joseph, it's to trust God. As Joseph says to his trembling brothers at the end of the Book of Genesis: "You meant evil against me; but God meant it for good." When we characterize God's activity as teaching us a lesson, more often than not, that's the lesson we come down to: "Have faith; it's going to be okay, sooner or later." Certainly that indefinite promise is not going to be much of a comfort to six million Jews killed in the Holocaust. Nor is it going to be much of a comfort to three thousand people who died in the World Trade Center and their families. But maybe it will provide some comfort. There is a great religious strength in many, many of those people.

John Horgan: I've talked to a lot of theologians about the problem of evil, and the only answers that I find at all satisfying suggest that God is not perfect; God is not this infinite, all-powerful, majestic, king-like being. You can find this notion of an imperfect God in the Kaballah, the Jewish mystical theology, and in Christian process theology. It also crops up in Gnosticism, a heretical Christian sect that flourished in the first few centuries after Christ. They all postulate in one way or the other that God isn't perfect. Of course, this is just another anthropomorphic concept of God, but it's an anthropomorphic concept that I find appealing, because it makes God more human, more like us. God is not omnipotent and all-knowing. God is somehow growing along with us. In some sense, our growth and anguish and difficulty are the same as God's; you can't separate the two. The poet Annie Dillard turned the phrase, "God, the semi-competent," to express this notion that God isn't perfect.

Frank Geer: I find that view very attractive. In a sense, what we're saying is that September 11 occurred because God matures his divine purposes through human contingencies; that the crack in cosmic reality that allowed September 11 to happen also opened up room for growth and change. As pattern-seeking creatures, we could even risk trying to figure out what growth and change might come out of September 11. For me, it gets back to our need to mature religiously so a more tolerant, loving practice of religion emerges across the board—in Christianity, Judaism, Islam,

Buddhism, Hinduism, all the various faiths, including New Age variants. People may start to realize that the primary value of religion has to be tolerance and understanding and cooperation, not only among their own group, but other faith groups.

John Horgan: Absolutely.

Frank Geer: The idea that September 11 happened because we needed to learn about what we believe is attractive to me, and maybe it's attractive to you. It's not going to be attractive to the husbands or wives or daughters or sons of the three thousand people who lost their lives on September 11. They're going to say that there must have been a better way to get that message across.

John Horgan: The way you put it makes it sound too deterministic. It still implies that there is an omnipotent God in control. What I was trying to suggest—and what process theologians and others have suggested—is that maybe God isn't fully in control. This takes away the notion of God as the ground of being, as a kind of ultimate foundation or security blanket that we can rely on. This means that God to a certain extent is struggling and floundering in the same way that we are.

Frank Geer: But you are also implying that things don't "just happen." You are moving away from saying that what happens is all just luck to the idea of an imperfect God, of a God whose power is not limitless. I was taking that notion a step further and thinking about how it might be applied to what happened on September 11. You hear over and over again—from the media, from individuals, from pulpits in churches and mosques and synagogues—that September 11 changed everything. What is it that changed? And how might things change for the better? But you're saying that whatever is happening may be happening without God managing it like the conductor of an orchestra. You're leaving room for human free will.

John Horgan: Yes, according to this heretical tradition, things are to some extent beyond God's control; he doesn't know what's going to happen either. The notion of a "semi-competent" God suggests that God is challenged by human events such as September 11 to change himself. As I recall, the Biblical story of the Flood can be interpreted this way. After destroying every creature in the world except for the passengers of the Ark, God promises that he will never again punish humanity with this kind of global extinction. God seemed to realize after the Flood that he had treated us too harshly. He needed to be more compassionate toward us, just as we need to be more compassionate toward each other. When you get too detailed with a theology like this, it can end up sounding silly. But the point is to make God even more human, especially compared to the stern, judgmental, almighty God of many parts of the Bible.

XIII
WHERE WAS SATAN ON SEPTEMBER 11?

WHERE WAS SATAN ON SEPTEMBER 11?

John Horgan: Do you think that the concept of supernatural evil, embodied by Satan, for example, is useful? Does it play any part in your thinking or help you address the problem of evil?

Frank Geer: When the word *Satan* first comes up in the Bible, it just means *that which opposes me*. So the concept of Satan refers to anything in your life that opposes you. If you're walking along a path in the woods and you stumble over a root and you trip and fall, you curse that root by saying, "Satan, be gone." That root is Satan because it opposed you; it's kept you from doing what you want to do.

Early on in the Biblical story, Satan is always an outside force, and so you get these horrible stories where thousands of Philistines are disemboweled and Samson takes their foreskins back to show his wife. Those Philistines are Satan. We're trying to occupy the land of milk and honey, to build our nation, and those are the people that oppose us. They have no value, they have no worth. We destroy them because they're Satan, that which is outside of us, which is keeping us from accomplishing our goal.

Later on in the Biblical story, *Satan* refers to people who are part of our nation who don't agree with us. Instead of Satan being the Philistines, Satan is the people of Israel who don't agree with you—the objects of the prophets' wrath and chastisement. Satan isn't the outsiders anymore; Satan is part of the nation. And then the final stage is that Satan becomes part of ourselves; Satan is the part of me that I can't live with. So you have that progression of that which you can't abide getting closer and closer to the center of who you are. Now that's how I understand Satan. I see Satan as functioning on all those levels at the same time.

John Horgan: So Satan is both external and within us?

Frank Geer: Let's say I need to get to a meeting and the subway doesn't come. Satan is keeping that subway from coming. Satan is also my enemies, who are out to keep me from accomplishing what I want to accomplish. Satan is also friends who are trying to drag me down, and Satan is the parts of myself that are working against me all of the time. So I've got four complementary satanic dimensions functioning at the same time. I'm not saying that Satan was driving that plane on September 11 or that Satan caused all this horror to happen. My understanding of Satan forces me to come to terms with the part of me that's on that plane carrying out a plan to destroy fifty thousand innocent people. To adapt Pogo's battle report from the Vietnam War era: "I have met Satan—and he is me."

John Horgan: So, in other words, we should resist the idea that Satan is something that is completely external to us.

Frank Geer: The question we've been asking is, "Where was God on September 11?" You could also ask, "Where was Satan on September 11?" I think if you ask that question, you need to look at those four categories or levels at which Satan could be said to exist.

John Horgan: There are some theologies that make Satan necessary. This Hindu guru named Ramakrishna was once asked about the problem of evil. Why is there so much suffering and anguish? Why is life so difficult? Why are there things always getting in our way? Ramakrishna's answer was that we need evil to thicken the plot. If we don't have difficulty, hardship, even to the point where we're hanging on by our fingernails, there's no plot, there's no drama to our existence. Life would be too boring.

Frank Geer: You were talking earlier about a God who doesn't manage things, a God who is not out to manipulate everything. You didn't actually say this, but maybe it's also a God who is aware in an ultimate sense of the process that we're all going through, and a God who in some way shares that awareness with us, and tries to point us toward better ways of overcoming our problems.

John Horgan: What you're saying reminds me of something that Elie Wiesel wrote about in one of his books about the Holocaust. He describes this scene at Auschwitz, where the Nazis have hanged two men and a boy in front of the whole camp. The boy is so light that he doesn't immediately die; he just slowly strangles. And one of the Jews in this crowd of inmates whispers, "Where is God?" And Wiesel thinks to himself, "God is up there hanging from that rope." Again, that's the only way I can make sense of the concept of God. If there is a God, he has to be a God that suffers.

Frank Geer: So maybe on September 11 God was in those people jumping from the top stories and holding hands as they fell to their death; God was in the heart and soul of every one of those people as they rode the building down as it imploded into dust and rubble. God was in the heart and soul of every one of those policemen and firemen after helping twenty-six thousand people escape as the buildings collapsed around them. God was in every wife, every child, every mother, every father of one of those firemen or victims who died as they struggled with their grief and tried to continue with their lives. That's a powerful articulation—but for me not entirely satisfactory, because it sort of makes God into the cosmic patsy.

John Horgan: Yes, it makes God look like too much of a victim, and it doesn't express the totality of our humanity, either. We don't just suffer; we have good times in life too. We have a tendency to reach out to God and to some ultimate meaning when the most awful things happen to us. But any real meaningful notion of God has to encompass the best things that happen to us, too.

XIV

AN EARTHQUAKE IN INDIA

AN EARTHQUAKE IN INDIA

John Horgan: Terrible traumatic events in which thousands of people lose their lives take place all the time around the world. How was September 11 different from or similar to those tragedies?

Frank Geer: Actually, September 11 was the second enormous tragedy that I witnessed in the same year. The other was an earthquake that took place in the state of Gujarat in India in January of 2001. I was in southern India then visiting a friend in Kerala. My friend runs a school, but on that particular day there was no school. It was an Indian holiday, National Day, January 26. That morning I was in my room reading a book and my friend came in. He looked like death; his face was ashen. He said there had been a terrible earthquake up in Gujarat, about three hundred miles away. Most of the housing in this area was not built to withstand such an earthquake, and so there had been thousands and thousands of casualties.

Over the next few days, all the communities in India galvanized themselves and began sending search-and-rescue teams to Gujarat. More than twenty thousand people died, which is seven times more people than died here on September 11. In addition, 167,000 people were injured and almost one million homes were destroyed. Thousands of people were pulled out of the debris still alive over the next four or five days because of the rescue effort. When the World Trade Center collapsed, by contrast, almost everyone was immediately killed. Anyway, this earthquake in India and the country's response to the disaster was in an eerie way a preview of what happened here in New York City after September 11.

John Horgan: After this earthquake, did the people in India ask, "Where was God?"—or whatever the equivalent question would be for a Hindu or Muslim?

Frank Geer: They didn't in those first few days, as far as I could tell. It would be interesting now to go back to Gujarat and ask, "How are you coping with this? How is this affecting your faith?" What I witnessed in the four or five days after the earthquake was this incredible concern and effort to save those who could be saved. There's a real similarity between that concern and what I witnessed at the World Trade Center, when the construction people told me that they wanted to make sure that no one else would die. In India, you could sense the entire nation dedicating itself to the task of saving everybody that was still alive.

John Horgan: I would imagine there would be a different emotional response to an earthquake, which can be seen as a pure act of God, as opposed to a terrorist attack.

Frank Geer: This rescue effort even went beyond India. Gujarat is a state that borders Pakistan. Of course, there are terrible tensions between India and Pakistan. But after the earthquake, people in the villages in Pakistan that border India offered their help, and at first the Indian government refused it. My sense was that many Indians—both Hindu and Muslim—were outraged by that decision, and so the next day the government of India accepted Pakistan's offer, and many Pakistani crews came across the border and helped.

John Horgan: So here was another example of a terrible crisis helping people transcend their differences.

Frank Geer: These traumatic events can help us move to a new level of understanding, tolerance, and cooperation. But unfortunately people may also become even more entrenched in their own ways. When people are threatened and frightened, they may have a harder time dealing with uncertainty, and often what they're looking for is a religious system or philosophical system that gives them answers without ambiguity. But systems that give you answers—without struggle, without toil, without ambiguity—can be very dangerous; if not for you, then for your neighbor, who may fall into the role of Satan.

XV
TAKING RESPONSIBILITY FOR OURSELVES

TAKING RESPONSIBILITY FOR OURSELVES

John Horgan: Let me try again to stand up for the scientific or non-religious point of view for a moment. It seems to me that the primary benefit of not believing in a supernatural order or plan is that we're forced to take responsibility for ourselves. We accept that there is no guarantee of our survival. We have infinite freedom to screw things up as well as to make things better. The only way we're going to be saved is if we save ourselves. Science tells us that we're here not because of some divine plan; we're here for some mysterious reason that nobody will ever understand. Science takes away the security of religion but it gives us freedom. It also forces us to take responsibility for facing all the threats to our survival.

I worry that our belief in God and a supernatural plan or order lets us off the hook; it makes it easy to be a fatalist. If we're just following a plan created by God, it doesn't really matter what we do; the plan unfolds with or without us. For example, the religious sensibility might lead you to accept an earthquake as an act of God that you can't really do anything about. But, actually, you can drastically reduce the harm caused by earthquakes by constructing stronger buildings. Even if we accept that there are limits to the human condition, we can do a lot to make things better for ourselves, if we take responsibility for ourselves.

Frank Geer: So the existential world-view says: "No one out there is going to take care of you. So if you want things to get better, you'd better get to work." The Christian world-view says: "You are saved just because you exist and because your Creator loves you. So get to work." Christianity does not say, "You're saved, so you're off the hook." Christianity says, "You're saved because you're loved, so get to work." And I guess the sad thing is that most Christians usually don't bother to get to work to make the world better. The equally sad thing is that most people who have an existential world-view don't bother either.

John Horgan: Yes. They look out for themselves.

Frank Geer: The Christians don't bother because of a sense of complacency, maybe; and the existentialists don't bother because of a sense of despair. In either response, we're just not getting it.

John Horgan: If there is any positive outcome of September 11, it may be that it has shocked people into taking their lives more seriously and looking at their lives in a broader context. That's true whether you're an atheist, pagan, existentialist, Christian, or Muslim. I hope that will be the enduring consequence of this event—rather than its leading to some terrible religious war, which is certainly a possibility.

Frank Geer: I like the idea of September 11 shocking people into trying harder to shake off complacency, despair, and intolerance; into trying to be more creative in addressing our problems. That doesn't mean it's okay that September 11 happened. It's not going to bring back those three thousand people or heal the wounds that young and old, rich and poor, black and white Americans are carrying with them. But it may help change things for the better.